Ocean Friends

ELEPHANT SEALS

Maci Dessen

PowerKiDS press

New York

Published in 2016 by The Rosen Publishing Group, Inc.
29 East 21st Street, New York, NY 10010

First Edition

Editor: Caitie McAneney
Book Design: Katelyn Heinle

Photo Credits: Cover, p. 1 (elephant seal) Mlenny Photography/Vetta/Getty Images; Cover, p. 1 (landscape backdrop) Giedriius/Shutterstock.com; cover (series logo coral vector design) Koryaba/Shutterstock.com; back cover mycteria/Shutterstock.com; pp. 3–24 (interior coral vector design) etraveler/Shutterstock.com; p. 5 Wild At Art/Shutterstock.com; p. 6 creativex/Shutterstock.com; pp. 9, 24 (flipper) David Osborn/Shutterstock.com; p. 10 elnavegante/Shutterstock.com; p. 13 (main) Eduardo Rivero/Shutterstock.com; p. 13 (inset) Frances Twitty/E+/Getty Images; p. 14 fotogestoeber/Shutterstock.com; pp. 17, 24 (pup) worldswildlifewonders/Shutterstock.com; p. 18 Filipe Frazao/Shutterstock.com; p. 21 Anton_Ivanov/Shutterstock.com; p. 22 Polryaz/Shutterstock.com.

Library of Congress Cataloging-in-Publication Data

Dessen, Maci, author.
  Elephant seals / Maci Dessen.
      pages cm. — (Ocean friends)
  Includes index.
  ISBN 978-1-5081-4168-6 (pbk.)
  ISBN 978-1-5081-4169-3 (6 pack)
  ISBN 978-1-5081-4170-9 (library binding)
  1. Elephant seals—Juvenile literature. [1. Seals (Animals)] I. Title.
  QL737.P64D47 2016
  599.79'4—dc23
                              2015023505

Manufactured in the United States of America

CPSIA Compliance Information: Batch #BW16PK: For Further Information contact Rosen Publishing, New York, New York at 1-800-237-9932

CONTENTS

Elephant seals are big ocean animals. Males have long noses like an elephant.

The male elephant seal's nose helps it make loud calls.

Elephant seals use **flippers** to swim. They have fat on their body called blubber.

flippers

Southern elephant seals are the largest seals in the world. They live in warm waters.

Male elephant seals are really big. Some are longer than a minivan!

minivan

Female elephant seals
are smaller. They don't have
long noses.

Elephant seal mothers
have one baby at a time.
They're called **pups**.

Elephant seals live in a group called a colony.

Elephant seals swim far to look for food. They swim very deep.

Elephant seals spend most of their time in water. They love to swim!

WORDS TO KNOW

flipper

pup

INDEX

C
colony, 19

F
flipper, 8, 9

N
nose, 4, 7, 15

P
pup, 16

WEBSITES

Due to the changing nature of Internet links, PowerKids Press has developed an online list of websites related to the subject of this book. This site is updated regularly. Please use this link to access the list: www.powerkidslinks.com/ocea/elep